LOST LEWE

Photographs by James Cheetham 1854
reproduced from the original glass ne

Is this James Cheetham's wife and children standing at the gate of 15, St. Anne's Crescent? Deeds show that number 15 was sold to 'Mrs E.J. Cheetham' in 1905 for £380. The family had previously rented 6, St. Anne's Crescent.

KIM CLARK

S.B. Publications

To my husband, Terry who realised the importance of these splendid photographs and arranged for their rescue.

First published in 2002 by S. B. Publications,
19 Grove Road, Seaford, East Sussex BN25 1TP

ISBN 1 85770 241 7

Designed and typeset by CGB, Lewes
Printed by Tansleys The Printers
19 Broad Street, Seaford, East Sussex BN25 1LS
Tel: 01323 891019

CONTENTS

Front cover: Everyone in Fisher Street appears to be dressed for some formal occasion and some important people have just arrived in their limousine. They seem to be heading for the police station (out of shot). We don't know the event – it is possible that this was connected to the visit of Princess Henry of Battenburg in 1910 when she opened the Victoria Hospital. James Cheetham always appeared more interested in the bystanders than the celebrities. A dog is well to the fore – dogs appear in many of his photographs. A charabanc waits outside Beards Brewery. There were at least 40 pubs in Lewes at the time, but respectable women never went in pubs and the town was full of teashops as well. There is one halfway down Fisher Street – the well-dressed ladies are strategically placed for refreshment when the excitement is over!

ACKNOWLEDGMENTS

The author would like to thank the following for all their help, without which this book would not have seen the light of day:

Brian Thompson, who saved the original negatives. Robert Prance, who copied all of them onto transparencies. John Eccles, who insisted on publishing some of them in the Sussex Express. They were seen by Steve Benz of SB Publications who phoned me at 8.30 in the morning on the day the first pictures appeared. This book is the result. Postcard collector, Mike Green, who identified the photographs as being the work of James Cheetham and who supplied vital information about him. Rendell Williams, who made available for comparison purposes his large collection of Cheetham postcards and provided more vital information. He also kindly gave permission for the use of four of his postcards in this book. Bob Ellison, who pointed out details that helped date the photographs. Norman Funnell, who identified Fanny Tester as his aunt and also supplied copies of family birth, marriage and death certificates that were invaluable. Mrs Marie Bassett, who identified members of the Salvation Army Band (see page 75) and Sue Fenwick, secretary to the Governor of HM Prison, Lewes, for additional information about the prison. Thanks also to the staff at the East Sussex Record Office and the Brighton Local History Library for all their help and Brigid Chapman for supplying additional information.

The story behind this book

Some years ago workmen renovating a cottage at Glynde found a box of glass negatives in an outhouse. They were thrown into the skip but fortunately one of the men, Brian Thompson, rescued them. A few nights later, in the British Legion club, Brian was talking about his find to the late Bill Ryall and their conversation was overheard by my husband, Terry. Recognising their possible significance, he took the fragile negatives and a friend, Robert Prance, copied them onto transparencies.

There were eighty-seven negatives – virtually all of photographs taken in Lewes or Offham over a period of some thirty years, the earliest being about 1904. When some were reproduced in the *Sussex Express*, Barcombe postcard collector Mike Green identified them as the work of James Cheetham. Further confirmation came from Rendell Williams of Southdown Avenue, Lewes, who has a large collection of Cheetham postcards. Many of the views on the glass plates were new to him but he had, in the form of postcards, a number that were similar. What did surprise him was that there were so very few downland views in the Glynde collection. 'It is certainly not a random sample of Cheetham's work,' he said. 'A great many of his photographs feature the downs with teams of oxen at work, cattle grazing and sheep cropping the grass.'

James Cheetham was forty-one when he came to Lewes from Ipswich in 1895 with his twenty-six year old wife, Mary Jane, and their two young children, to work at HM Prison as clerk and assistant schoolmaster. One of the first things he did was join the Lewes Camera Club, which was then meeting at the Fitzroy Library. He was admitted to membership in

1896-97 and the handwritten entry reads: 'J Cheetham. HM Prison Lewes (in red ink) 5s' followed by his address at 6, St. Anne's Crescent. He is in the membership list each year until 1900-01, when there is a note by his name 'pd Oct 1900'. The next list of members appears 1906-7 but Cheetham was then not among them.

James Cheetham was a superb photographer, as the plates on the following pages show, and by this time he may have been regarded as a professional photographer, causing him to leave the 'amateurs only' Lewes Camera Club. Around 1905/6 he stopped producing proof cards stamped CHEETHAM–LEWES so presumably by then he had established sales outlets for his work. He also gave up captioning them in handwriting directly on to the negative and instead applied ornately printed strips of information to each print. However he retained his position at Lewes Prison.

In 1905 the family ceased to be tenants of 6, St. Anne's Crescent and became owner occupiers of nearby number 15. The purchaser of the property was, surprisingly, Mary Jane, perhaps using some money she had inherited. James Cheetham retired from the prison service in 1917 but lived until 29 June 1941 when he died, aged 87. He was, a Roman Catholic but unusually for a catholic was buried in St Anne's churchyard. The registers of St Pancras church, where he had worshipped and was for some years secretary of its Benevolent and Thrift Society, show all other burials around this time were in the extra-mural cemetery of Lewes. When his widow died on 31 January 1947, aged seventy eight, she was buried in this cemetery.

The Chalk Pit Inn, just outside Lewes at Offham, appears in the background of a series of photographs of the family pictured on the rear cover. There was no indication of the families identity but some detective work revealed that in 1903 Harry Tester held the licence of what was then a beerhouse at Chalkpit Cottages. He died, aged fifty-three, in 1917 and the licence was transferred to his widow, Fanny. When the slides of this family appeared on the screen during an illustrated talk I gave at Lewes Town Hall in November 2000 a voice called out: 'That's my Aunt Fanny'. In the audience was Norman Funnell, former Captain of Tableau, Captain of Effigies and now a Life member of Cliffe Bonfire Society. He knew Fanny as the wife of his uncle, William Funnell, who, when a young man, had worked in the timber haulage business that Harry Tester ran as well as the beerhouse. When Harry died William moved in to Chalkpit Cottages, initially perhaps to help run the beerhouse. Seven years later, on Boxing Day, 1924, in spite of a twenty year differences in their ages, William married the sixty year old Fanny. They left the Chalk Pit and went to live in St. Pancras Gardens, Lewes, next door to William's elderly father.

The relationship seems to have scandalised the Tester family. Fanny lived to be 90, dying in 1955. Norman Funnell thought that Fanny was childless, but this was not the case. Harry and Fanny were married in January 1885 at the Catholic Church of the Sacred Heart at St. Pancras, Lewes, the same church that James Cheetham attended. By 1891 they had two children, Lily Florence born in 1886 and Harry William born in 1889. Their daughter Lily is shown in several of the prints. In 1908, also on Boxing Day, she married a young man from Lewes with the unforgettable name of Ethelbert Larkin. Before Harry's death the family appears to have been close knit and several photos show Fanny and Harry with Lily and her young family.

Harry Tester was illiterate at the time of his marriage. Most, if not all, of his life was spent at Offham. His father's name was Moses, a most unlikely name for a Catholic.

Fanny was also born at Offham. Her maiden name was Tourle. Presumably a Catholic family, the Tourle's probably came from the Buxted area. Fanny went to school and at the time of her marriage was working as a domestic servant at Firle, possibly at Firle Place. Her second marriage took place at Southover Church, Lewes, so she seems to have abandoned her earlier Catholicism.

What connection, if any, was there between James Cheetham and the Tester family? Perhaps it was little more than a casual friendship with Fanny, struck up through attending the same church. Or was Cheetham in the habit of dropping in to the beerhouse at Offham for a drink when out walking on the Downs with his camera seeking the pastoral shots of which he was so fond? Perhaps we shall never know – any more than we will know why a box of his glass negatives was gathering dust and cobwebs in an outhouse at Glynde.

Regrettably old postcards fade and the detail is often poor. The negatives found at Glynde show the superb quality of Cheetham's photography. Some are badly foxed and it has been necessary to crop the edges before reproducing them on the following pages. Others have been left as they are because trimming would have resulted in too much of the photograph being lost. Even so, they give far more detail than do many old postcard reproductions. In just two cases negatives were too damaged to be used. Because they represent areas of Lewes that would otherwise have been unrepresented, Cheetham postcards of similar views, kindly loaned by Rendell Williams, have been used instead.

Unlike many photographers pursuing their profession or hobby before, during and after the First World War, James Cheetham's photographs are full of life. He likes to show children playing, deliveries taking place, a car coming down the street. Dogs are frequently in the frame but the days when they could sit in the middle of almost any road in Lewes have long gone. Most of the locations are themselves little changed, but the atmosphere that Cheetham portrayed went long ago. Truly these photographs are of a 'Lost Lewes'.

Kim Clark,
East Street, Lewes
January 2002

Lewes prison was opened in 1853. James Cheetham started work there in 1895. Both sexes were held in in the prison and women prisoners were allowed to keep their babies with them. The 1891 census records three babies living at the prison. In 1917 the prison was effectively closed and Cheetham retired. It reopened (for male prisoners only) in 1931. This photograph, dated 1905, would have been taken from the garden of Winterbourne House then occupied by Lewes solicitor Augustus Fitt Drake. It was demolished in the 1960's.

A pre-1914 view of the prison from Landport Bottom. Only the base of Shelley's windmill now remains. The turf is studded with flowers and the schoolboys in their best Eton collars are obviously looking at something, possibly the racing stables in Spital Road. The Victoria hospital, opened in 1910, is in the background.

After many years as arable land, Landport Bottom was bought by Lewes District Council and returned to grassland. The dewpond in the immediate foreground was restored in 2001.

St Anne's Hill in about 1906. Cattle are being driven on the hoof to the weekly livestock market which had been transferred in 1879 from the High Street to a site opposite the railway station. The barber's shop on the right is displaying the traditional red and white banded pole which represents the ribbon bound round a patient's arm before bleeding. There is a horseman coming down the hill and a dog on the pavement. Cheetham seems to have been fond of dogs – they appear in many of his pictures.

The Pelham Arms on St Anne's Hill has been extended since this photo was taken, probably in the 1920's. The inn was sold by the Earl of Chichester in 1799 to Richard Williams, clerk to Lewes racecourse, and became the meeting place of the racing fraternity of the town. A later licensee was retired jockey Thomas Read, who numbered among his customers the 19th century's most famous jockey, Fred Archer.

Lewes Old Grammar School moved from Southover Grange to this house on St Anne's Hill in 1718. The building had been the Chantry House of St Peter's church (long gone) and was bought by a wealthy benefactor and given in trust to the grammar school. The premises were re-built in 1885 from which time the present school ceased to have any connection with the free school founded by Agnes Morley *c*1512. The building is little changed today but the railings have gone – removed in the Second World War. It is a winter picture, so the creeper is without leaves.

St Anne's Hill in summer. It became fashionable, in the late Victoria era, to cover the bare bricks, stone or flint of one's town house with climbing plants and here the front elevations of Tyne House, The Corner House and the south-west facing side wall of St Wilfred's House, are almost totally obscured by luxuriant creepers.
One of Cheetham's characteristic dogs stands idly in the empty street. A fire warning beacon can be seen in front of St Wilfred's house.

The earliest of three photographs showing the Town Clock mounted in 1881 on the school house of St. Michael's Church in the High Street. This photograph shows the original Georgian frontage of the Brewers Arms. Horace Graham was the landlord at that time.

Children have hoops, prams and a handcart. A telegraph boy is in the foreground. A sign says 'Baths 6d'. These baths were part of Dusart's, a chemist's shop and hairdresser. This was taken after the original building of Dusart's was burned down in 1904. The Edwardian building, shown in the photograph is now 84/85 High Street. Number 84 has green tiles around the side entrance and this must have been the entrance to the bath house.

Roughly the same period as the previous picture but the baths now have a sign saying 'Electricity'. Next to St Michael's church is the photographic studio where Edward Reeves started his career in the 1860s. The business has remained in the family ever since and the studio, unchanged since this photograph was taken, is now run by his great-grandson, Tom.

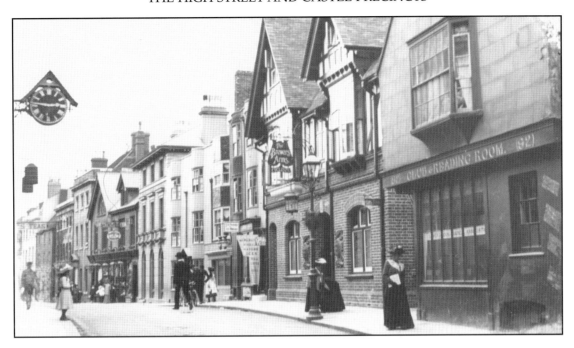

This was taken a little later than the previous two pictures. The Brewers Arms has been re-built and carries a 'cyclists welcome' sign. Bull House, where radical visionary Tom Paine, author of *The Rights of Man* and *The Age of Reason* lived, is keeping his memory alive as the reading room and the headquarters of the Lewes Radical Association. It is now occupied by the Sussex Archeological Society. Teas, coffee and ices are on offer at Willoughby's tea-rooms, later the Tatler tea rooms that closed in the 1980's.

The Barbican, showing the Gun Garden and, above it, Castle Lodge. When the Sussex Archaeological Society succeeded the Freemasons as tenants of Lewes Castle in 1850 the open area in the photograph, then known as the Castle Yard, was 'cluttered up with a large shed, a room in the temporary occupation of the Grammar School and one used for some years, rent free, by the Infant School'.

By 1854 the area had been cleared and became known as the Gun Garden from the Russian gun that was on display there. This gun was obtained by Lord Panmure, the Secretary of State for War, when an application was made by the town in 1857 for some trophy of the Crimean War to mark the fact that 300 Russian prisoners were detained in Lewes during that conflict. Woolwich Arsenal even made a Russian gun carriage for it. Some prisoners never returned home and were buried in St John's churchyard.

In this fine photograph, probably later than the previous shot, the gun has been repositioned and Castle Lodge has acquired more creeper – and a new owner.

The Sussex Archaelogical Society, which had hired it from 1885 to house its valuable library, was given notice to quit in 1904 by Charles Dawson, one of its more prominent members, who had bought the lodge the previous year.

Dawson, who died in 1913, was associated with the discovery of the remains of Piltdown Man, which was claimed at the time to be the lowest known form of human being – *Eoanthropus dawsonii*. The Piltdown skull was proved to be a fake and Dawson was almost certainly responsible for the hoax.

The Barbican, about 1908. An early morning shot, when the light would have been right, catches the newspaper van delivery to Castlegate House, then owned by novelist and playwright Frank Frankfort Moore. In 1924 the house was acquired by East Sussex County Council for use as a clinic. Generations of Lewes babies were weighed here and received their free cod liver oil ration. It has now reverted to private use.

High Street and the White Hart about 1908. There is no War Memorial at the top of School Hill. There are deep blinds outside Morrishes the drapers and the neighbouring shoe shop. The shoe shop was owned by Mr Russell and was the first shop in what became the chain 'Russell and Bromley'. Next door is the Town Hall, once the Star Inn. During the Marion Persecution seventeen protestant martyrs were held in its medieval cellar before being taken outside and burnt. At the top of Market Street are the premises of Addison the stationer, agent for the Britain and Foreign Bible Society.

Around 1914. The White Hart is much smarter now, with palm trees on its first floor balconies. Small boys gather round the motor cars outside the hotel and a chauffeur keeps a watchful eye on them. If his passengers were staying overnight at the White Hart he would have been accommodated at the Unicorn Inn next door. Roof advertisements are popular – Marsh's Dining rooms stands out. The same family ran the butcher's shop on the corner of Station Street, now the Abbey National Bank. 'Ye Olde Tobacco Shoppe' was a prominent landmark until the end of the 60's. It was owned by Alderman Hubert Woolmore, Mayor of Lewes in 1962.

School Hill about 1914. The bush in the foreground by the flagpole is a pomegranate. It is still there, outside the solicitor's office at Trinity House, and its scarlet flowers add a touch of colour to the street scene in autumn. In the left foreground is Braughton House, a girls school that closed in the 1950s. Its last headmistress was Miss L A Way. This Cheetham postcard, loaned by Rendell Williams, has exactly the same perspective but is a few years earlier than the glass negative from Glynde which was too badly foxed to reproduce.

The charred remains of the 300 year-old Bear Inn, after the disastrous fire which destroyed it on the 18th June 1918. It took the combined efforts of four brigades nearly five hours to get the blaze under control. The cause of the fire has remained a mystery.

Boats could be hired from the Bear and the landing stage escaped the fire. On the corner is Rice's, selling cycles, petrol, oil and grease as well as saddlery. It caught fire eight times, but each time fireman were able to douse the flames before they could take hold.

This view of Cliffe High Street is much earlier than the Bear fire picture and Rice is not yet catering to the motor age. Rice remained on this site until the early 60's, reverting to its core business of saddlery and cycles. It moved to the other side of the bridge before closing in the 1970's. Cuilfail does not exist in this picture. The fine barrow visible on Cliffe Hill is now obscured by vegetation. This is another instance in which the negative was too damaged to reproduce and Rendell Williams has again come to the rescue with an almost identical Cheetham postcard.

This photograph of Cliffe Square, taken in the 1930's, is one of the latest in the collection. There seems to be very little traffic for the policeman to direct. Shaw's stores and other buildings on the left-hand side were demolished to make the small car park by Cliffe Church. On the opposite side are the Malling Drapery store and Moore's (perhaps one business). Signs advertise 'Big Value' from the 'Lewes Miscellaneous Stores'. The business was also a pawnbroker denoted by the three balls sign hanging near the chimney. Just visible is a direction sign for Lewes Golf Club.

Another sunlit empty road and a teashop. Malling Street in the 1920's. The sign of the Wheatsheaf Inn is clearly visible. The building is still there but is now a private house. Next door is the County Town mineral works (burned down in the 1960's), formerly the South Malling Steam Brewery owned by Elmsley & Co. The brewery closed in 1898 and the premises were taken over by J. F. Philips to make mineral water. The cottages on the left of the street are long gone – the Esso garage occupies the site. The downs are kept bare by grazing sheep – they are now covered in trees and bushes.

Just one pedestrian in this unusually empty Cheetham shot of Malling Street in the 1920's. Malling Street has changed more than most parts of Lewes. In the foreground is the burial ground of St. Thomas, Cliffe. This disappeared in the 1970's when Malling Street was widened and the Cuilfail tunnel opened. The cottages on the right were also lost. The fine bowfronted Georgian house on the left was demolished to make way for the Esso garage.

Malling Street again – this time coming in from the north. Standing out against the wooded hillside above the former South Malling Steam Brewery is the white gable of Undercliffe House. In the 1950s it was occupied by Pete and Pru Mason, a local couple who adopted an American Wild West life style. In full cowboy regalia, they would ride in tandem round the town on their golden Palomino horse, tethering him outside any shop from which they wished to make a purchase. The horse trough was removed in the 1900's.

This photograph was taken from Malling Hill before 1914. The fields are now covered by housing and a large industrial estate. Almost all the houses along Spences Lane have been demolished. Spences House was then owned by the Rickman family. Hannah Rickman (died 1905) was rather eccentric. The clearly visible mound was the grave of her favourite horse, Charlie. There was a spiral path leading to an enclosed area with a granite slab and Miss Rickman climbed to the grave each day. In the background is Church Lane, running down to a long-gone barn and cottages.

An unusual shot of Malling Mill, which burned down in September 1908. The three-storey building on the right is the Mill House. Apart from the mill, all the other buildings are still there but both sides of Mill Road are lined with houses and the cornfields have disappeared.

This view of the river would have been taken from the track leading up to the present site of the golf club clubhouse. There is a goods train at the sidings and in front of them is a large area of neatly tended allotments. The original course of the river can be clearly seen behind Wharf House in the right-hand foreground. The area known as 'The Island' was formed when Cliffe Cut was made in 1795. The old river course rejoins the Ouse just before the gasometers. It remained open until 1961. Filling it in may have contributed to the extensive flooding that the South Street area experienced in October 2000.

A panoramic view across Lewes from the castle. The Martyrs Memorial stands out against the downland turf but today the Cuilfail estate covers the hillside below the memorial and mature trees almost obscure it. This photograph must have been taken shortly before the first houses were built for a line of trees has been planted and the road marked out. The trees were cherry plums and a few still remain. A road leads up from Chapel Hill but there is no golf club-house at the top.

Lewes before the Landport and Neville estates were built. On the skyline are the stands of Lewes Racecourse. Allotments, in the middle distance, cover some of the fields of Richard Brown's Landport Farm. By the river Stricklands warehouse stands out, with a second warehouse, now Vipers Wharf, nearer to Cliffe Bridge. Both are now converted to residential use. In the foreground are the gasholders of Lewes Gasworks, a company set up in 1822. The gasometers were removed in the 1970's and houses built on the site.

A closer view of the railway sidings and the gasometers. The wooded area is the garden of Leighside, a large Victorian mansion that was the home of Quaker philanthropist and ship-builder, Burwood Godlee. The house, just visible in the trees, was demolished around 1914. The Railway Land Local Nature Reserve now occupies the site of the garden, railway sidings and allotments as well as the adjoining water meadows.

This view of Lewes Station from the castle was taken in 1904. One of the steam trains is at the London platform, the other is at the platform for Barcombe or Uckfield. Both lines were axed by Dr Beeching and the platform replaced by the station car park. A lane, now Mountfield Road, leads to a barn which still stands opposite the Leisure Centre. The water meadows to the left are now covered by the buildings of Priory School and Lewes Tertiary College.

The 'to' and 'from' Brighton platforms of Lewes station in the 1920s. The line to the left of the picture has been removed so passengers from Seaford and Newhaven no longer have to use the bridge (recently restored) when changing to a London train on the other side of the station. The train is a pushpull, used on lines where there was no turntable.

Grange Road in the 1920s – with only one parked car. Today, like almost all the residential streets in Lewes, it has cars parked bumper to bumper. It was after the new station opened in 1857 that there was a demand for housing in the area from Victorian commuters with business interests in London. The developers of the day obliged and Grange Road was soon lined with desirable residences.

About 1910, looking into Priory Street from Southover High Street. The view has hardly changed although the King's Head is no longer a Page and Overton's house. The object on the pavement is a fire warning beacon. An errand boy is on a delivery, perhaps to one of the fine Regency houses in Priory Crescent, opposite the pub. The railings in front have gone, as did so many others, to be turned into armaments in the Second World War.

Southover High Street before the first World War with a car driving along in the middle of the road. An artist sits on a doorstep sketching Anne of Cleves House. At that time Southover Manor, in front of which is a lamppost, would have been a private house owned by Frank Verrall's family. It later became a girls school and has now been converted into flats and its grounds covered by an estate of houses and bungalows.

A view of the north side of Southover High Street, showing the contrasting architectural styles. Unusually, for a Cheetham photograph, there is little sign of life except for the woman leaning rather awkwardly out of the sash window of a house aptly named the Gables. All these houses are little changed today.

The rear dorter of the Priory ruins in Southover with the castle perfectly positioned on the skyline in the gap between the trees. A similar view of the castle can be obtained today by looking through the eye slits of the massive helmet, erected in the Priory grounds as a memorial to the Battle of Lewes. The sheep-grazing pasture has given way to the courts of the Southdown Tennis Club, which now occupy most of the foreground.

St Pancras Road before 1910. Most of the fine flint wall disappeared when Cleve Terrace was built in the large garden that it once enclosed. The piece remaining has been breached by gateways and garage entrances. The cottages to the left have gone, replaced by flats after the floods of 1960. Fanny Tester lived in one of them, Number 44, with her second husband, William Funnell. He strenuously resisted attempts to rehouse him after the floods but his protests were to no avail. His cottage was demolished and he was rehoused in Winterbourne Lane where he died in 1978.

Looking down Mount Pleasant from the Fisher Street/West Street corner to the Elephant and Castle. One of the men in the group on the left is studying the handbills on the wall advertising forthcoming attractions and there is a large poster advertising Keatings flea powder – a popular pesticide until the 1950's. The police station is on the left and a deliveryman struggles up the hill with a heavy looking box on his handcart.

A classic Cheetham shot with a dog sitting casually in the roadway of Offham Terrace. Today this is part of the A2029 bringing morning and evening rush hour traffic to the town centre and the Phoenix Causeway river crossing. The pedestrian with the walking stick pauses at the entrance to St John's Terrace – perhaps deciding whether or not to drop into the Elephant and Castle.

The same view, and perhaps the same pedestrian, in summer just before the First World War. The Elephant and Castle is moving with the times and offering 'Good Stabling and Storage for Motor Cars'. A be-goggled and gloved motorist, his female passenger with her hat fashionably secured with a motoring veil, plus the boy in the back are in a smart tourer with the registration number AP 159.

A truly lost view of Lewes – the De Montfort municipal workhouse before 1910. It was built in 1868 as part of the Chailey Union and housed 250 inmates, the sexes being strictly segregated. The excessively neat gardens were tended by the inmates. The workhouse system was abolished in 1929. The buildings were pulled down in 1960 and flats built on the site. In the background the high brick wall surrounds one of the many racing yards that flourished in the town.

This view taken from Castle Precincts shows the parkland between the Avenue and Prince Edwards Road before the Park Road houses were built. The Avenue was originally known as D'Albiac Avenue after the family who owned the land it was built on. It was shortened to The Avenue at the request of residents who found the original name too much of a mouthful. In the foreground is the Paddock, still an open space and until recently, still partly used for grazing.

Two more des. res. have just been added to the Avenue, probably around 1907. Development of the Wallands area began in the 1870s and proceeded slowly. It had been parkland on the estate owned by the Shelley family, into which a George D'Albiac married in 1806. The closely grazed turf of the park is clearly visible and some of the original flint walls still survive as garden boundaries.

A horse, extreme right, grazes in the field opposite Bradford Road in 1911. This land, known as Baxter's Field, was also used as a sports field by the workforce of the printing firm from which it takes it name. Today it is still a sports ground and is now used by Lewes Grammar School.

The far end of the Pells lake, looking much more attractive when this photograph was taken than it does today. In 1897, when a Water Carnival was held there, it was described as 'a beautiful piece of ornamental water, fringed with trees…' The Environment Agency is currently spearheading an initiative to enhance the lakes with new plantings and other improvements.

Boating on the Ouse, upstream of Cliffe Bridge, before 1906. The angler with a roach pole lifts his line out of the water to get it out of the way of the oarsmen who would have hired their boats from the Bear Inn. The latticed bridge was known as Admiral Curry's bridge after the owner of Malling Deanery – it was later replaced by an iron suspension bridge. This was taken down in the 1960s and Wiley's Bridge built from the Pells to link the new Malling estate to Lewes. Len Wiley was a popular Lewes councillor.

Cheatham was fond of repeating shots in different seasons. Almost the same scene, photographed in 1923. It is no longer high summer, there is not a fisherman in sight, the children on the bank are well wrapped up against the cold, and the one boat on the water must be privately owned, as the Bear Hotel had burned down five years previously.

Looking downstream on the righthand bank of the river to the Pells in 1905. The Pells swimming pool and lakes lie behind the poplars and other trees in the background. The haystacks and buildings on the right could be those of The Old Farmhouse, which survives to this day behind Talbot Terrace, although completely surrounded by terraced housing. The fields have remained undeveloped, but have now largely reverted to marshland.

The same spot but looking in the opposite direction towards Offham. The towpath along which, in 1839-41, horses towed barges laden with materials to build the Balcombe viaduct, can still be followed on foot, with difficulty in places, to Ryelands Bridge, the limit of the Upper Ouse Navigation.

Talbot Terrace, 1914. Some of the 10,000 soldiers billeted in Lewes before being sent to the front, pose for the cameraman. These young men are wearing 'Kitchener Blues' walking out uniform and the two girls on the left are clearly impressed. A delivery van, advertising Hovis, stands outside the local bakery.

Toronto Terrace on a snowy day – and again unusually for a Cheetham shot, not a soul in sight. Rendell Williams has a postcard which shows exactly the same view but with a uniformed man, perhaps a station master, standing outside his house on the corner. He must have found it too cold to hang around for a second shot!

This photograph of a military camp at Houndean Bottom would have been taken in July 1910 when several thousand territorials were sent to the area to take part in combined manoeuvres. The volunteer soldiers were under canvas all around Lewes for some ten days. The horses in the foreground indicate that a mounted regiment is encamped here. Volunteers brought their horses with them.

Lewes Races in the 1930s. Runners line up at the start of the mile race but one of the horses in the group next to the two by the rails appears to be giving his jockey a bit of trouble. The racecourse opened in the 1720s, a grandstand was erected by subscription in 1772 and it saw its last race in 1964. It is still used as training gallops.

Development on the downs. The first houses on the Neville estate – North Way in 1930. To which has since been added South Way, Cross Way, East Way and a whole lot more. The road to the racecourse stands out. Nowadays trees and bushes largely obscure the line of the road. The remaining sheep grazing land, known as Landport Bottom, was ploughed during the Second World War but has now been restored to chalk pasture by Lewes District Council which acquired the land.

Offham Church photographed in 1909, less than sixty years after it was built by the Reverend George Shiffner. The Shiffners of Coombe Place were one of the largest landowners in the locality. Elder sons traditionally served in the British Army and the younger ones often became rectors of Hamsey. Every war between 1815 and 1945 seems to have claimed at least one Shiffner baronet.

The original parish church at Hamsey is still used for occasional services. It stands on an isolated hilltop well away from the modern village.

Offham House. This fine Georgian House would have been owned by Mrs Charrington before the First World War. The sundial on the pediment is similar to the one on Dial House near Cliffe Bridge in Lewes. The house is unchanged today and now belongs to the Goodman family

Looking from Offham hill across the Ouse valley. Ousedale House, opposite the Chalk Pit Inn, still has its unusually shaped flowerbeds. Across the fields, Chalk Pit Cut runs from the river to a wharf at the foot of the hill. A tramway, still to be seen today, ran from the yard of Chalk Pit Cottages down to the wharf 150ft below.

Harry Tester looks over the farmyard gate at Chalk Pit Cottages. As well as running the beerhouse, Harry kept livestock and ran a timber haulier business. His marriage certificate shows he was illiterate and Fanny probably kept the books for him. The beerhouse would have originally catered for workers at the chalk and lime works. By the time Harry took over the licence in 1903, the wharf below would have closed.

This photograph of Lily Tester feeding the hens would have been taken in 1905. Was it at the request of Fanny that the parrot in its cage features in the photograph? The bird was her prized possession and when it died she had it stuffed and kept it in the front parlour. Amazingly, it still survives and is now in the front room of Norman Funnell's house in Windover Crescent, having been left to him by his Uncle William, Fanny's second husband.

Harry Tester, timber haulier, at work in 1910. Harry with his long carter's whip, stands by the lead horse and young William Funnell sits with arms folded on the load. This photograph was taken on the Offham Road leading into Lewes, in front of where the Landport estate is today. Were the trees killed by Dutch Elm Disease? The disease is known to have occurred before the extremely severe strain that decimated elms in the 1970's and 80's.

The Tester family in about 1912. Lily Tester married Ethelbert Larkin in 1908. Although Harry is smoking his pipe, he appears to have made some effort to smarten up for the camera. Both Fanny and Lily have taken a great deal of trouble over their hats!

Norman Funnell has some other photographs of the Larkin family. However he was unaware that they were Fanny's grandchildren. His memory is that Fanny described Ethelbert as 'someone who worked with Harry'. Was there a family rift after Fanny's second marriage to William Funnell?

Judging by the age of the children, this shot can have been taken only shortly after the previous one. However Harry does not seem to have tried at all. Note the string around his knees and the roughly secured trousers. Fanny is definitely not amused!

'Your carriage awaits, m'lady'. Fanny is dressed to impress, Harry still with his trousers tied below the knees with twine. The smart turnout is a buggy and it is fully fitted up for road work with mudguards and oil lamps. Is it perhaps a new acquisition?

Off at last, but it is just a trot around the chalkpit. Norman Funnell possesses a postcard of this view addressed to Fanny in 1913. There is no inscription. Possibly Fanny sent it to herself.

The chalk and lime works closed in the 1870's. In the Testers time the floor of the pit was used for grazing. Now it is overgrown with bushes.

The lych gate of St Anne's church, Lewes. 'The largest and by far the most perfect church now remaining in Lewes,' wrote William Figg in his *Memorials of Old Lewes* (SAC vol 13). It is only in comparatively modern times that it has been known as St Anne's. It was originally St Mary's Westout and its parish was united with that of St Peter's in the sixteenth century.

Although a Roman Catholic, James Cheetham seems to have had a strong affection for St Annes and took many photographs of it. He is burried in the graveyard.

This is one of the earliest pre-1910 Cheetham photographs of the interior of St Anne's church, splendidly decorated for a processional service. It shows the inscription round the chancel from The Revelation 7,12: *'Blessing and glory and wisdom and thanksgiving and honour and power and might be unto our God for ever and ever.'*

Another view of the interior of St Anne's, with the inscription absent from the re-decorated chancel arch. The chancel itself was rebuilt in the thirteenth century and the roof dates from 1538 when the parishes of St Mary's Westout and St Peter's were amalgamated.

The church of St Pancras in 1906 – one of the very few photographs taken by James Cheetham of his own church. From the days of the Marian persecution, when seventeen Protestants were burnt at the stake outside the Star Inn, Lewes Roman Catholics were without a church of their own for some 300 years. Services were first held clandestinely and later more openly in a house at Southover.

However, when the Church of the Sacred Heart and St Pancras was opened on 25 January 1870 a crowd of around 1,000 angry protesters had to be restrained from riot by the police. Harry and Fanny Tester were married here in January 1885. This view is from a card lent by Rendell Williams.

When this photograph of Lewes Salvation Army Band was published in the *Sussex Express* Marie Bassett of Blois Road, Lewes, recognised some members of her family. Seated, left, is her grandfather, Isaac John Payne, and centre is Bandmaster Bevin. Standing, from left are her uncles Frederick and Eric Payne, fourth from left is Harry Nye and with the drum is Arthur Lusted.

Where was this photo taken, and what was the occasion? The stepped wall is distinctive and it could be the Weslyan Chapel in Station Street, now used as an antiques market. The teacher in her little cap is rather behind the times for 1930, the probable date of the picture. Some of the children are certainly still around. Perhaps one of them will be able to give more information.

This beautiful photograph by James Cheetham of Offham church in its downland setting appeared in the July 1932 issue of the *Sussex County Magazine*. Together with another typical Cheetham study of cattle on the banks of the Ouse it illustrated an article by James Turle entitled *Where Cobbett Rode*. The credit – *Photo: J Cheetham* – appears beneath the two pictures in this quality county magazine which was published from 1927 to 1956.

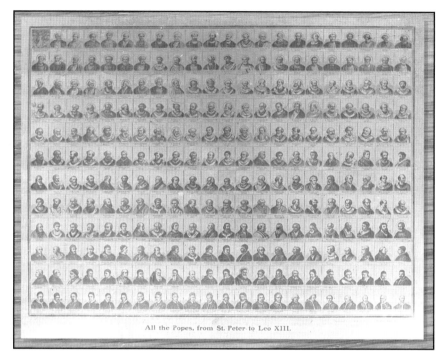

All the Popes, from St. Peter to Leo XIII.

All the Popes. Why, one wonders, did James Cheetham take the trouble to pin this page of thumbnail pictures of Popes from St Peter to Leo XIII to a board and photograph it. A devout Catholic, Cheetham never photographed the Lewes Bonfire processions. Even today banners are slung across Cliffe High Street proclaiming 'No Popery' and effigies of Pope Paul V are burned by Cliffe Bonfire Society.

A sad postscript posing yet another question. Why did James Cheetham photograph 'Sass' Fenton's grave? Had he been asked to do so by the family or was she perhaps a relative or friend?

There was no indication of where this photo was taken and it was by chance that the author stumbled over the grave in Lewes cemetery.

Sarah Hannah Fenton and her husband John, a grocer's assistant, lived in New Road, Lewes for many years and she died in Brighton, of cancer, at the age of forty-six. Research yielded the details of her life and death but it was not possible to find any connection between the Fentons and James Cheetham.

BIBLIOGRAPHY

Brent, C and Rector W. *Victorian Lewes* Phillimore 1980

Cairns, Bob. *Lewes in old picture postcards.* European Library – Zaltbommel/Netherlands 1988

Fleming, Barbara. *Lewes, Two Thousand Years of History.* S B Publications 1994

Godfrey, W. *A History of Lewes.* Lewes Borough Council 1933

Holter, G. *Sussex Breweries* S B Publications 2001

Poole, Helen. *Lewes Past.* Phillimore, Chichester 2000

Pocock, David. *Pesthouse Field.* St Anne's Crescent Residents Association 1996

Smith, V, edit. *The Town Book of Lewes 1837-1901* Sussex Record Society

McCarthy, Edna & Mac. *Sussex River, Journeys Along the Banks of the River Ouse.* Lindel Organisation Ltd. 1979.

Young, Bill in association with Bob Cairns. *Lewes Then and Now.* SB Publications 1998

Middleton, Judy. *Lewes in Old Photographs.* Alan Sutton 1990

Lewes Camera Club membership book at ESRO

Sussex Archaeological Collections, vols 13, 68

Sussex County Magazine, vol 7

Kelly's Directories of Sussex 1890 to 1934

Pikes Lewes, Newhaven and Sussex Directory 1906 to 1951–2